Girls'
SOFTBALL

by Brian Howell

GIRLS'
SportsZone

Published by ABDO Publishing Company, PO Box 398166, Minneapolis, MN 55439. Copyright © 2014 by Abdo Consulting Group, Inc. International copyrights reserved in all countries. No part of this book may be reproduced in any form without written permission from the publisher. SportsZone™ is a trademark and logo of ABDO Publishing Company.

Printed in the United States of America,
North Mankato, Minnesota

052013
122013

THIS BOOK CONTAINS AT LEAST 10% RECYCLED MATERIALS.

Editor: Chrös McDougall
Series Designer: Marie Tupy

Photo Credits: Aspen Photo/Shutterstock Images, cover, 1; Elaine Thompson/AP Images, 5, 7, 8, 41; Fernando Llano/AP Images, 11; J.P. Wilson/Icon SMI, 13, 14, 16; The Oklahoman/Nate Billings/AP Images, 19; Sue Ogrocki/AP Images, 21, 29, 37; Mike Ehrmann/Getty Images, 23; Frederic J. Brown/AFP/Getty Images, 25; Parkersburg News & Sentinel/Jeff Baughan/AP Images, 26; Knoxville News Sentinel/Wade Payne/AP Images, 30; Dustin Snipes/Icon SMI, 33; Elaine Thompson/AP Images, 35; Columbia Daily Tribune/Matthew Cavanah/AP Images, 38; The Oklahoman/Sarah Phipps/AP Images, 42; Red Line Editorial, 44

Library of Congress Control Number: 2013932500

Cataloging-in-Publication Data

Howell, Brian.
 Girls' softball / Brian Howell.
  p. cm. -- (Girls' sportszone)
 ISBN 978-1-61783-990-0 (lib. bdg.)
 Includes bibliographical references and index.
 1. Softball for girls--Juvenile literature.   I. Title.
 796.357--dc23

2013932500

Pitching with Cat Osterman

Australia's hitters had no answer for Team USA pitcher Catherine "Cat" Osterman at the 2008 Olympic Games in Beijing, China. The hitters reached for pitches curving to the outside. They swung under pitches that sailed high. And they swung over pitches that dropped.

Osterman recorded 21 outs in the game. Thirteen of those were strikeouts. And Australia did not get any hits. Osterman was nearly flawless in leading the United States to the 3–0 victory.

The pitcher from Houston, Texas, throws hard. But Osterman has always dominated hitters with the movement on her pitches. That is exactly what she did in throwing a no-hitter against Australia.

Team USA's Cat Osterman throws a pitch against Australia during the 2008 Olympic Games in Beijing, China.

"I think we mixed a lot more curveballs than normal because they were either going after my drop or laying off of it, and that's normally my go-to [pitch]," said Osterman, who starred on the US national team from 2001 to 2010. "We had to adjust and [I] threw a few more rise balls and curves, but it worked."

SUPER STAR PITCHER

Jennie Finch was one of the best pitchers in Team USA history. During her career, Finch helped Team USA win an Olympic gold medal in 2004 and a silver medal in 2008. She was also a three-time All-American at the University of Arizona. Finch always practiced great pitching mechanics. That included proper grip of the ball, with three or four fingers, depending on the size of the pitcher's hand. "Pitching mechanics are crucial, not only to get the most out of your body, but for safety," said Finch, who retired from the National Pro Fastpitch league in 2010.

A drop ball is a pitch that comes in fast but drops before reaching the plate. A rise ball is a pitch that increases its elevation as it moves to the plate. A curveball fools hitters because it curves in toward the hitter or away from the hitter. Osterman has been a master at these pitches. At no time was that more on display than in the Australia game.

Osterman ended the first inning with an inside pitch that caused the Australia hitter to back away from the plate. But the pitch sailed over the inside part of the plate for a strikeout. In the second inning, Osterman struck out two hitters. She then ended the third inning with a great rise ball. The Australian hitter swung and missed for another strikeout.

Osterman never let up. In fact, she seemed to get better as the game went on. In the seventh and final inning, she struck out the first two hitters. She was just one out away from a no-hitter. Then Osterman delivered a low breaking ball that produced yet another strikeout.

Osterman has never overpowered hitters with speed, like some pitchers do. Instead, she learned the art of pitch movement. She proved that in the win over Australia.

Cat Osterman celebrates with her US teammates after throwing a no-hitter against Australia in the 2008 Olympic Games.

"I actually don't throw a fastball," Osterman said. "A curveball, a rise ball, and a drop ball are my main three [pitches]."

Osterman found success as a pitcher right away. As a 10-year-old, she got an opportunity to fill in as a pitcher for her youth league team. She struck out one of the first batters she faced. "I asked for pitching lessons for my 11th birthday," she said. "I struck out one person and I loved it."

Osterman was a dominant pitcher at Cypress Springs High School in Texas. From there she went on to star at the University of Texas. She became the only player to be named the USA Softball Collegiate Player of the Year three times. She also led the Longhorns to three College World Series appearances.

Cat Osterman of the United States throws a pitch against China during the 2008 Olympic Games.

In 2012, Osterman was still fooling hitters. She was the ace pitcher for the USSSA Pride of the National Pro Fastpitch league.

Pitch Movement

Great pitching is one of the keys to softball. After all, every play starts with a pitch. As Osterman proved against Australia, a dominant pitcher can defeat a great team of hitters. Good pitchers are able to throw the ball past hitters for strikes. It is difficult to hit the ball well against a great pitch. So when a batter does make contact, it often goes to a fielder for an out.

Great pitchers are all different, though. Some rely on a powerful fastball. Others don't throw very hard. Pitchers like Osterman find success with off-speed pitches that move a lot. And some pitchers can dominate by using a combination of speed and movement.

RICKETTS RULES

Keilani Ricketts is an exceptional pitcher who combines speed with movement. The University of Oklahoma pitcher was named the USA Softball Collegiate Player of the Year in 2012 as a junior. In 2009, she was named the EA Sports/ESPN Rise national high school Player of the Year. Ricketts is also a member of the US national team. Her fastball has been clocked at 73 miles per hour. It isn't just speed that makes Ricketts good. When Ricketts throws, the ball moves so much that hitters have a hard time finding it.

Quick Tip: Achieving Pure Spin

Putting proper spin on the ball can help a pitcher develop great off-speed pitches. When Cat Osterman was learning to pitch, she would put electrical tape around the ball, creating a perfect line on the ball. Then, when she practiced her pitching, she tried to throw so that the ball would spin in a way that she could see the line the whole time it was in the air. Seeing the line—without any wobbles—let her know she had pure spin on the ball. "The more pure your spin is, the more sharp your movement is," Osterman said.

Osterman has always believed in ball movement as the best way to get outs. "Speed is not everything," she said. "I'm on the slower end of the spectrum, but the fact that I move it and I have the good combination of enough speed but enough movement is what's gotten me to where I am. I think people need to focus on their spin and their movement more than anything."

Putting movement on the ball is all about the grip. The way a pitcher grips the ball determines the direction in which it spins. Then the speed of the spinning determines how much the ball moves. Players add more spinning speed by snapping their wrists just before releasing the ball.

Movement in pitching is now more important than ever. In 2009, the pitching circle in high school softball moved from 40 to 43 feet (12.2 to 13.1 m) from home plate. That makes power pitching less effective.

"Pitchers now are doing very well working their spins and keeping the ball in play and making the defense make some plays," said Bobby Pacheco, former coach at St. Mary's High School in Arizona. "There aren't a lot of overpowering pitchers now, but what the 43 feet has done to the pitching schemes is pitchers are coming back with more spins, more technique, and being more effective."

That has been Osterman's philosophy for years.

Cat Osterman of Team USA prepares to throw a pitch against Japan during the 2010 world championships.

chapter 2

Slap Hitting with Caitlin Lowe

S tanding in the batter's box, Caitlin Lowe rested the bat on her left
shoulder. She stared at the pitcher standing 43 feet away. When the
pitcher went into a windup, the left-handed Lowe raised the bat to
get it ready. Then, standing with her feet shoulder width apart, Lowe began
her signature swing.

She stepped to the left with her right foot. Then she crossed her left
foot over her right as she shuffled to her right. With another step, she
swung the bat and slapped the ball toward the shortstop. Within seconds,
Lowe was standing on first base with yet another hit during the 2009
Canada Cup.

Team USA's Caitlin Lowe has proven to be one of the best slap hitters in the world.

Lowe is well known as one of the best hitters in the sport. What has made her most effective is her perfection of the slap hit. The slap gives a batter a running start toward first base. That makes it more difficult to throw her out. Lowe has great speed and has used that to her advantage throughout her career, especially when using the slap.

"Most people know her as one of the best slappers in the world, if not the best," said Lauren Lappin, one of Lowe's teammates with the USSSA Pride.

Lowe's all-around ability with the bat has allowed her to get on base a lot. She is exceptional at bunting and full swings, as well as slapping.

Team USA's Caitlin Lowe hits against China during a 2008 game in Oklahoma City.

"I'm very impressed with her ability to do almost whatever she wants, and very few players have that," said Larry Ray, who was an assistant coach at the University of Arizona when Lowe was an All-American for the Wildcats. "If Caitlin struggles in one area, she always has another strong area to fall back on. That's a rare combination."

Lowe has always had a rare combination of skills. The Californian was an All-American in high school before her stellar career at Arizona. As a Wildcat, Lowe won two national titles. Then she went on to play for the US national team at the 2008 Olympic Games. Lowe said she has always had a love for softball.

"I have a degree in psychology, but my passion is softball, and if I can be involved in that, and I can make my living that way, whether it's playing, teaching, whatever it may be, there's where my passion lies," said Lowe, the 2012 Player of the Year in the National Pro Fastpitch league.

SLAPPING TO A RECORD

Kayla Braud is one of the best hitters in the country. The University of Alabama leadoff hitter and extraordinary slapper helped her team win the 2012 NCAA championship. Before getting to Alabama, Braud had a national-record 103-game hitting streak at Marist High School in Oregon. "In high school, I didn't hit away a lot," she said. "I mostly slapped and bunted." At Alabama, Braud became a great all-around hitter.

The Slap Hit

In softball, a player can get on base either by getting walked or by getting a hit. There are a lot of ways to hit the ball. Some hitters like to drop the ball down for a bunt. Some hitters are great at putting a good, solid swing on the ball and driving it to the outfield or over the fence for a home run.

Finding success as a slap hitter is a unique skill. It takes a great deal of coordination to be a good slapper. The hitter must be able to swing the bat

Caitlin Lowe of Team USA steps into a slap hit against Canada during the 2010 World Cup of Softball.

while shuffling through the batter's box. She must have a good read of the strike zone. The hitter also has to connect with the ball just right.

"Slapping is something that's not overpowering," said Kayla Braud, a talented slapper and the leadoff hitter for the University of Alabama, which won the 2012 national championship. "You're not trying to kill it. You're trying to hit it to the right spot. The goal is to [have the bat swing] on a plane and hit the top of the ball and get a nice hop. You don't want to hit it hard, just nice and smooth. It's an art, really."

Slap hitters typically start from the left side of the plate. That puts the batter closer to first base. When slapping, a batter gets a running start toward the base. Usually, slappers are fast players who are great at making contact with the ball. When most hitters would just be starting to run to first base, a slapper is often a step or two on her way.

Lowe is one of the greatest slap artists in softball. She said the key to being successful is getting comfortable with the unique motion of slapping.

POWER AND FINESSE

US national team member Michelle Moultrie was the Southeastern Conference Player of the Year in 2012. Her ability to beat opponents with a powerful swing or a slap hit makes her the most dangerous type of hitter. "If you could ask me what I'm looking for, I'm looking for Michelle Moultrie, a left-handed hitter that can hit for power, drop a bunt down, slap a ball into a hole," said Tim Walton, Moultrie's coach at the University of Florida.

Quick Tip: Footwork

All great slap hitters know that correct footwork is key to a successful hit. Players can practice their footwork at home or on the field. Just make sure there is enough room to move. First, get into a standard batting stance. Then step back with the right foot. Next comes the crossover step. This provides the hitter with the explosion needed to hit the ball. Cross over with the left foot and swing the bat. Continue practicing that motion and it will become more comfortable.

"The hardest part about slapping is hitting in basically a pretzel position," she said. "So, if you can make yourself comfortable with that contact point then you're going to be able to run through and do it easier."

Years ago, slapping wasn't a weapon seen very often. Today, it is one of the biggest weapons in the game. A good slap hitter, like Lowe, can make a big impact on the game. Lowe can get to first base in 2.6 seconds after slapping the ball. That helps her get on base more often.

"It has its place in our game and I personally think it's exciting," said Stacey Nuveman, who was a great power hitter at UCLA in the late 1990s. "Slapping is unique and different, but it's undeniably consistent and effective. Baseball purists might not like it, but they can't argue [the fact] that it works."

Brianna Turang of the University of Oklahoma slaps a single during a 2011 game.

chapter 3

Catching Pitches with Ashley Holcombe

Crouched low behind home plate, Team USA catcher Ashley Holcombe awaited the pitch from teammate Jackie Traina. The first pitch was a bit high. Holcombe snagged it and turned her glove downward. "Strrrrrike!" yelled the umpire.

The second pitch touched the outside corner of the plate. Holcombe squeezed it in her glove and turned her hand to the inside. "Strrrrrike!" yelled the umpire. Two pitches later, the Australian hitter swung and missed for a strikeout. Traina got credit for the strikeout during the championship game of the 2012 World Cup of Softball. Yet most pitchers agree that a great catcher who knows how to frame pitches plays a key role in getting strikes.

Team USA catcher Ashley Holcombe, *left*, reacts after a Japan batter struck out during the 2011 World Cup of Softball.

Holcombe has been doing that for years. Born in Fayetteville, Georgia, Holcombe began playing softball at four years old.

"Catching is my passion in softball," said Holcombe, who was an all-state player all four years of her high school career. "I take a lot of pride in it because I feel like that's where I can contribute most to the team. A lot of it is about passion back there and having the heart. I feel like I am very passionate and enthusiastic behind the plate."

Holcombe went on to star at the University of Alabama. She is now considered one of the best catchers in the world. Holcombe and other great catchers can make a huge impact on the game. They help to decide which pitches will be thrown. A strong-armed catcher can throw out runners on the base paths. One of the most important skills for a catcher is framing. That is the art of making pitches look like strikes to the umpire.

WILLIS SHINES BEHIND PLATE

Pro softball standout Megan Willis has been one of the top defensive catchers in the sport for years. She proved that during her career at the University of Texas, from 2004 to 2007. Willis had the best fielding percentage (.994) for any catcher in Texas history. She was the Big 12 Conference defensive player of the year in both 2006 and 2007. "I started catching when I was younger because I liked getting dirty," she said. "As I've gotten older, I've realized I love being in the middle of everything."

It is a skill Holcombe has mastered. Against Australia, Holcombe sat confidently behind the plate and caught Traina's pitches. They worked together to trick batters and record strikes.

In the sixth inning, Keilani Ricketts was pitching. Holcombe continued her great work. Ricketts needed one more strike to finish the inning. She threw a hard pitch on the outside corner. Holcombe caught it and slightly turned her glove to the inside. "Strrrrrike three!" yelled the umpire.

Another pitch, another strikeout for Team USA.

Team USA catcher Ashley Holcombe, *right*, looks to make a play against Canada during the 2011 Pan American Games.

Framing Pitches

A dominating pitcher can help a softball team win a lot of games. A good catcher who knows how to frame pitches can make a pitcher a little more dominant.

"Framing is huge," said Holcombe, who has been on the US national team since 2009. "I take great pride in my framing. You can help your pitchers get more strikeouts in a game. [Pitchers] may not realize it at a young age, but as they get older, they'll realize that their catcher is really helping them expand that strike zone."

Pitching strategy begins before the pitch is thrown. First the pitcher and catcher work together in deciding what pitch to use. They decide whether the pitch should be fast or slow, inside or outside. Then the catcher sets up to the side of the plate where the pitch is designed to go. Finally, the pitch is released.

Many times the batter will swing at the pitch. When the batter does not swing, the umpire determines whether the pitch was a strike or a ball. That is where the catcher's job becomes more important. Some pitches are obviously out of the strike zone. Some are obvious strikes.

On questionable pitches, the umpire needs to make a quick call. The better the pitch looks after it gets to the catcher, the more likely the umpire is to call it a strike. Framing the pitch by moving the glove slightly after catching it can be the difference.

Holcombe was behind the plate for 10 Team USA strikeouts during the 2012 World Cup of Softball championship game. Several of those were

Team USA's Stacey Nuveman, *left*, frames a pitch that goes for a strike against North Korea in a 2006 game.

called third strikes. That meant the batter did not swing, and Holcombe had to squeeze the ball and sometimes sell the strike to the umpire.

Holcombe said the first thing a catcher needs to learn is to be relaxed behind the plate. Limiting movement, especially arm movement, is crucial to good framing. The more movement an umpire sees, the less likely he or she is to call a strike. When Holcombe catches pitches, she does so with a straight arm and a stiff wrist. She catches the outside of the ball and turns it slightly toward the plate with her fingers.

"Just a little curl. Not a curl of my wrist, just a little curl of my fingers because it's limiting the movement," she said.

This high school catcher frames a pitch during the 2011 West Virginia state championship game.

Quick Tip: Learning to Frame

When practicing her pitch framing, Ashley Holcombe focuses on one side of the ball. For inside and outside pitches, she said, "I want to try to think about catching the outside of the ball." For a high pitch, Holcombe focuses on the top of the ball. "You don't want to catch it straight up because it's going to appear higher in the strike zone, and it's going to take your arm back and there's no chance the umpire is going to call it a strike."

Megan Willis has been a great catcher for years. She worked with star pitcher Cat Osterman at the University of Texas and for the Florida Pride in the National Pro Fastpitch league.

"When going out and receiving the pitch, number one, I want you to think about catching the ball so the ball is facing home plate," Willis said. In addition to turning the ball to the plate, Willis said body movement plays a key role in selling pitches, too.

"Think about getting your nose and your shoulders behind the pitch," she said. "If that ball takes you a little bit farther to the inside or to the left, not only are you going to get your hand out there, but now you're going to shift your shoulders and nose behind it."

When a catcher is good at selling pitches, a softball team can get a lot of strikeouts.

Infield Defense with Lauren Gibson

T he University of Tennessee softball team was loaded with talent. That's why it qualified for the 2012 College World Series. As good as Tennessee was as a team, however, second baseman Lauren Gibson stood out.

"Lauren is a complete player in every aspect," Tennessee co-coach Ralph Weekly said. "She's what we call a five-tool player: she can run, hit, throw, field, and think. She does it all."

Gibson is just 5 feet, 6 inches (168 cm) tall. Yet she is a powerful hitter. She has come up with countless big plays on offense throughout her career. However, Gibson's slick fielding is just as impressive as anything she does with the bat.

The University of Tennessee's Lauren Gibson (27) attempts to turn a double play against the University of Arizona in a 2010 game.

That was shown in a 2012 game against the rival University of Kentucky Wildcats. Kentucky had a runner on first base. Gibson fielded a ground ball near the second base bag. She took two steps to her right and put a foot on the bag for the first out. Then she fired the ball to first base to complete a double play.

Gibson's all-around talent has been on display on the international stage, too. She has been the starting second baseman for the US national team since 2011. At the World Cup of Softball in 2012, Gibson's glove helped Team USA to a victory against Brazil.

Tennessee's Lauren Gibson, *left*, prepares to tag out an Oklahoma State University base runner during a 2011 game.

In the third inning, as the ball bounced on the infield dirt, Gibson positioned herself in front of it. The ball took a hop to the right. So did Gibson. She leaned over and reached down to scoop it up. After picking up the ball with her glove, Gibson grabbed it with her right hand and tossed it over to first base for an out.

Three batters later, a Brazilian batter hit a high hopper to Gibson. She fielded the ball chest high. Then she quickly threw the ball to first base for the last out of the inning.

Gibson has made a habit of making great defensive plays to help her team. She has gained a reputation as one of the best defensive infielders in the world. Gibson gives it her all on defense because she knows that making plays with her glove is important for her team. Tennessee and Team USA are glad to have her powerful bat and great glove on their side.

"Lauren is the epitome of a ballplayer," Team USA coach Ken Eriksen said. "She comes to play every day, she loves to practice, and those things lend themselves to long-term success."

A STANFORD STAR

From 2009 to 2012, Ashley Hansen of Stanford University was one of the best players in college softball. The 2011 USA Softball Collegiate Player of the Year combined great hitting with great fielding from her shortstop position. Hansen was the Pac-12 Conference Defensive Player of the Year in 2012. "She has been an outstanding player both offensively and defensively," Stanford coach John Rittman said. "She's the glue on our defense."

WATLEY DOES IT ALL

Natasha Watley made history in 2004 as the first African American to play for the US softball team at the Olympic Games. She helped Team USA win the gold medal that year. She also played on the silver-medal-winning team in 2008. Watley is now a professional player. She is an exceptional hitter and base runner. She's also a top defensive player at shortstop. "I think she's the best shortstop in the world," said Mike Candrea, who coached Watley on the US team.

Fielding Grounders

Behind many great pitching performances is often great fielding. That was the case in the 2012 Southeastern Conference semifinals. University of Alabama pitcher Jackie Traina was able to maintain a shutout in a 1–0 win over the University of Georgia.

"We're very fortunate to have Jackie Traina on our side, but the defense behind her was really, really good today," Alabama coach Patrick Murphy said.

Perhaps the most important defensive skill to learn is fielding ground balls. An infielder who knows how to successfully field ground balls can prevent a lot of hits and runs.

The first step to being a good fielder is to have no fear. Sometimes, the ball comes very hard and fast at a fielder. She can't be afraid to get in front of it and make a stop.

The next step is being in the ready position. This requires a fielder to have her feet square, her eyes on the ball, and her body ready to move in any direction. From the ready position, a good infielder must be able to react quickly when the ball is hit. From the ready position, a fielder also

Team USA shortstop Natasha Watley scoops up a ground ball during a 2008 game.

Quick Tip: Repetition Is Key

A simple way to give an infielder a lot of practice is to have another person roll ground balls to her. This allows the infielder to work on different types of ground balls and then complete the play with a throw. "The purpose for this is really to work on glove positioning, to work on footwork, and it really gives you a great opportunity to get a lot of repetition in a short amount of time," said Mike Candrea, coach at the University of Arizona and former Team USA coach.

has to be prepared to field a low ground ball or one that takes a high hop. That's why many of the best fielders have strong legs and good flexibility.

"Our goal with infielders is to make them look like the smoothest thing you've ever seen, like they're gliding on ice," said Patty Gasso, the coach at the University of Oklahoma. "We work a lot on quick steps and reactions. A lot of what we do is aimed at making sure our legs are strong enough so that we can move quickly from a ready position."

Getting to the ball fast is only part of the job. A fielder must know how to handle the ball, too. Fielders must be prepared to secure the ball with the glove and then transfer it to the throwing hand. Most infielders, including Gibson, practice their technique so that it's a smooth and natural motion from fielding the ball to throwing it.

After securing the ball, an infielder has one final difficult task—the throw. Sometimes, the fielder has time to set her feet and make a solid throw to the base. That's not always the case, however. Some plays could require an off-balance or hurried throw. Because of that, it's important to practice all types of throwing situations.

"We get them to throw at different angles to simulate the plays they're going to have to make during a game," Gasso said.

Practicing the fundamentals of fielding ground balls can make a good team even better. It certainly worked for Gibson and the rest of her Tennessee teammates. The Volunteers had the best fielding percentage in the nation in 2012.

Australia second baseman Sandy Lewis snags a grounder against Canada during the 2008 Olympic Games.

Base Running with Rhea Taylor

One of the great things about softball is that it puts a variety of skills on display. Some players have great power. Others are artists with how they pitch or field a ball. Then there are players like Rhea Taylor, whose pure speed makes her a star on the base paths. When she gets on base, which is often, she is a terror for opponents.

"She has the potential to be a game changer with her speed and ability to get on base," said Aaron M. Moore, the general manager of the Chicago Bandits of the National Pro Fastpitch league. Moore signed Taylor to a contract in 2012. Taylor also plays for the US national team.

Taylor is a great hitter. But it is when she gets on base that she does her best work. She played for Team USA at the 2012 World Cup of Softball.

Team USA's Rhea Taylor celebrates after scoring a run against Japan
during the 2011 World Cup of Softball.

Taylor got on base with an infield single against Brazil. Then in the blink of an eye she turned on her speed and slid into second with a stolen base. Moments later, she was on third base with another steal. Rhea went 3-for-3 with two runs and two stolen bases in Team USA's 9–0 win.

"I know my role. I know what I have to do," she said. "I have to get on base to help my team out. That's all I'm here for."

Taylor has excelled in her role for years. She was a three-time All-American at the University of Missouri. As a freshman in 2008, she

Rhea Taylor (3) jumps onto home plate after hitting a home run in 2011 while her University of Missouri teammates wait to celebrate.

was given the Golden Shoe Award. It honors the best base runner in college softball.

"She does things that you just don't see on the base paths," Missouri coach Ehren Earleywine said. He watched Taylor steal 184 bases during her four years as a Tiger.

Taylor discovered early on that her speed could be a great asset to her team. As a freshman at Missouri, she got on base often. Once she got there, she was instantly looking to get to another base.

"I have to steal second, because my job is to get on base and then steal second so the power hitters that come up, they can hit me in," said Taylor, who grew up in Georgia.

Stealing bases is not solely about speed, though. Good base runners also need to be smart. Even the fastest base runners have no chance to get an extra base in some situations. But for those who are fast and smart, like

SETTING THE BAR

During her career at the University of Georgia, Nicole Barber set a college softball record by stealing 73 bases in a row without being caught. She learned how to use her speed and great technique to become one of the best base stealers in college history. "She's a great base stealer because she's fast, and she knows how to be on time on the bases," said Lu Harris-Champer, Barber's coach at Georgia.

FENTON BREAKS RECORD

The University of Alabama won the 2012 college national championship. Jennifer Fenton was a big reason for that. The center fielder for the Crimson Tide broke University of Georgia star Nicole Barber's record in 2012 when she stole her seventy-fourth base in a row. She was thrown out on her next attempt. Fenton finished her career as one of the most successful base stealers in college history. She said timing was the key to her success. "Instead of watching the ball leave the pitcher's hand, I watch the pitcher's footing," she said. "I watch the back foot lift up and start from there."

Taylor, the stolen bases add up. Taylor stole a Big 12 Conference-record 57 bases as a freshman in 2008.

Taylor's speed and smarts have made her a dangerous weapon at Missouri, for Team USA, and now in the professional league.

Running the Bases

At first glance, it would appear that base running is an easy skill. As long as a player is fast, she should be able to be successful, right? Not quite.

In addition to speed, a good base runner needs to be smart. Sometimes a pitcher has a fast release or a catcher has a powerful arm. Stealing on them is not as likely to be successful. Good base runners also need to have a bit of an attitude and a belief that they won't get thrown out.

"When I'm at first about to steal second, I'm looking at the catcher thinking, 'I wish you would try to throw me out. I wish you would,'" Taylor said.

That confidence has led to a lot of steals by Taylor. Her all-around ability has been important, too. Sprinting the 60 feet (18.3 m) to second base and beating a throw to the bag is not easy. Taylor's natural speed gives her an advantage. But she has perfected the full art of stealing.

Unlike in baseball, a softball runner cannot take a lead off a base. In softball, a runner is not allowed to leave the base until the pitch leaves a

Team USA's Caitlin Lowe (26) takes off stealing behind a Taiwan infielder during the 2008 Olympic Games.

pitcher's hand. That makes the first step very important. An explosive first step off the base gives the runner an advantage.

"That can determine whether you're out or safe," Taylor said.

After the first step, the base runner relies on her speed to get to the next base in a hurry. Taylor is able to go from one base to the next in about 2.6 seconds. That makes it very difficult for a catcher to throw her out.

A great first step and blazing speed are crucial. The final piece to being a successful base stealer is the slide. A good slide can allow the runner to get her foot to the base before an infielder can apply a tag. Or the slide can help the runner get her foot underneath a tag and touch the base safely.

Missouri's Rhea Taylor, *right*, steals second base against Oklahoma State University during the 2010 Big 12 Conference tournament.

Quick Tip: Learning to Slide

Sliding into the base can be a fun part of the game for base runners. It can also be one of the most enjoyable skills to learn. Charity Butler is a softball instructor in Florida. She was a star at the University of Southern Mississippi from 2003 to 2006 before playing professionally. She said the best way for a player to learn how to slide is to practice on a Slip 'n Slide water slide. "They have a blast, they overcome a lot of fears without even realizing it, and then you can translate a lot of that to the field," she said.

University of Alabama speedster Jennifer Fenton has combined her speed with a great feet-first sliding technique.

"I think the key to her is she slides correctly, directly into the bag, and then uses a pop-up slide so that if the throw gets away, she's at third base before you can blink," Alabama coach Patrick Murphy said. "To me, that's a great technique for her. And it should teach young kids who are stealing bases to go directly into the bag and pop up."

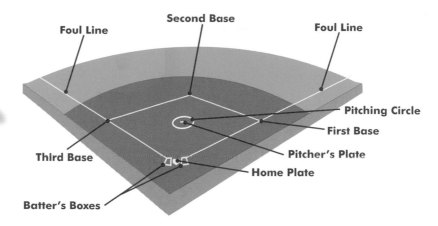

Foul Line
Second Base
Foul Line
Pitching Circle
First Base
Third Base
Pitcher's Plate
Home Plate
Batter's Boxes

bases

The bases—home plate, first, second, and third— are 60 feet (18.3 m) apart.

batter's box

A box, drawn in the dirt with chalk, in which a hitter must stand when it is her turn at bat.

foul lines

The lines that mark the side borders of a field.

pitching circle

A circle with an eight-foot (2.4 m) radius that surrounds the pitcher's plate.

pitcher's plate

A spot 43 feet (13.1 m) from home plate from which pitchers must pitch.

ace

>The best pitcher on a given team.

breaking ball

>Any pitch that is designed to have movement to fool a hitter, such as a curveball or drop ball.

bunt

>A technique used by a hitter in which she holds the bat and tries to tap the ball into play.

double play

>A play on defense during which two outs are recorded on the same play.

fielding percentage

>A measurement that shows defensive performance. It takes into account putouts, assists, and errors.

flawless

>Doing something without any mistakes.

fundamentals

>The basic rules or principles of a particular skill.

lead off

>When a base runner steps off the base to get a head start to the next base before a pitch is thrown.

no-hitter

>A game in which a pitcher does not allow a single hit to the other team.

strikeout

>An out recorded when the pitcher gets three strikes on a hitter.

strike zone

>The area directly over home plate and between a batter's armpits and knees. A pitch thrown here is a strike.

umpire

>A person who is on the field to enforce the rules of the game.

glossary

Selected Bibliography

Buckheit, Mary. "Slap-hitting Trend Strikes Oklahoma City." *ESPN.com*. ESPN Internet Ventures. 12 July 2005. Web. 4 April 2013.

Gardiner, Andy. "USA's Cat Osterman Pounces with No-hitter vs. Australia." *USA Today*. USA Today. 13 Aug. 2008. Web. 27 Feb. 2013.

Hays, Graham. "Caitlin Lowe Builds Her Life around Softball." *ESPN.com*. ESPN Internet Ventures. 21 June 2012. Web. 27 Feb. 2013.

Strange, Mike. "Animal Cages to Batting Cages, Lauren Gibson a Hitter." *GoVolsXtra.com*. Scripps Interactive Newspapers Group. 11 May 2011. Web. 27 Feb. 2013.

Further Readings

Brazier, Roanna, and Kathy Veroni. *Coaching Fastpitch Softball Successfully*. 2nd ed. Champaign, IL: Human Kinetics, 2005.

Finch, Jennie, and Ann Killion. *Throw Like a Girl: How to Dream Big and Believe in Yourself*. Chicago, IL: Triumph Books, 2011.

Garman, Judi, and Michelle Gromacki. *Softball Skills & Drills*. Champaign, IL: Human Kinetics, 2011.

Hsieh, Lawrence, and Michele Smith. *Coach's Guide to Game-Winning Softball Drills: Developing the Essential Skills in Every Player*. Camden, ME: International Marine/Ragged Mountain Press, 2008.

Walker, Kirk. *The Softball Drill Book*. Champaign, IL: Human Kinetics, 2007.

Web Links

To learn more about softball, visit ABDO Publishing Company online at **www.abdopublishing.com**. Web sites about softball are featured on our Book Links page. These links are routinely monitored and updated to provide the most current information available.

Places to Visit

National Baseball Hall of Fame and Museum
25 Main Street
Cooperstown, NY 13326
(888) 425-5633
www.baseballhall.com

Softball has its origins in baseball. This hall of fame and museum highlights the greatest players and moments in the history of baseball.

National Softball Hall of Fame and Museum
2801 NE 50th Street
Oklahoma City, OK 73111
(405) 424-5266
www.asasoftball.com/hall_of_fame/

Opened in 1957, the hall of fame is a tribute to the history of softball and many of its former star players. More than 360 people have been inducted into the hall of fame. The museum is located at the ASA Hall of Fame Complex, which is the frequent home of the US national team and Women's College World Series.

ABOUT THE AUTHOR

Brian Howell is a freelance writer based in Denver, Colorado. He has been a sports journalist for 20 years, writing about high school, college, and professional athletics. In addition, he has written books about sports and history. A native of Colorado, he lives with his wife and four children in his home state.